Original title:
Hidden Paradise

Copyright © 2024 Book Fairy Publishing
All rights reserved.

Editor: Theodor Taimla
Author: Karoliina Kadakas
ISBN HARDBACK: 978-9916-756-20-1
ISBN PAPERBACK: 978-9916-756-21-8

Arcadian Hideaway

In fields where dreams dissolve away,
Soft whispers of the wilted hay,
The skies embrace the fleeting day,
And twilight yields to shadows' play.

A brooklet hums a soothing tune,
Beneath the gilded arc of moon,
While fireflies in merry strewn,
Compose a lune of endless swoon.

Embrace the hollow, hear its song,
A refuge where we both belong,
Our hearts in sync, a pulsing throng,
In Arcadia, we grow strong.

Uncharted Oasis

A hidden jewel in desert dunes,
Where life rebirths in countless boons,
Between the stars and sunlit noons,
The dance of flowers gently tunes.

An echo of the ancient breeze,
Whispers through the date palm trees,
Respite found in moments' seize,
In sands that cradle timeless ease.

Beneath the shade of verdant hues,
The world takes on a brighter muse,
As night surrenders to the dews,
The oasis' charm makes tales peruse.

The Untouched Reserve

A tranquil realm where silence reigns,
Untouched by time's relentless chains,
Where every path unseen constrains,
And nature's peace forever gains.

The forest hums with ancient lore,
A symphony in each uproar,
The harmony we can't ignore,
As leaves from yesteryears encore.

Boundless greens of elder days,
Guardians of the secret ways,
Preserve the light in hidden rays,
Till dawn revives the dormant gaze.

Elusive Eden

Beyond the gates of dream, we find,
A paradise within the mind,
Where gentle winds and leaves entwined,
Form Eden's realm, forever kind.

The rivers flow in crystal streams,
Through meadows bright with sunlight beams,
In every corner, nature gleams,
Reflecting our most cherished dreams.

A haven where the heart can rest,
Within the cradle of the blessed,
With every breath we feel possessed,
By Eden's touch, we are impressed.

Mystic Lands

In the realm where dragons fly,
Whispers ride upon the breeze.
Stars align in emerald skies,
Secrets held in ancient trees.

Wonders float on silver streams,
Crystal waters gleam and wane.
Time dissolves in cryptic dreams,
Mystic lands where legends reign.

Echoes of forgotten lore,
Mingle with the twilight's song.
History speaks forevermore,
Worlds unknown yet timeless, strong.

Sleeping Eden

In the gardens, night descends,
Softly cloaked in moonlit charm.
Silent dreams, the twilight sends,
Eden safe from worldly harm.

Petals glisten, pure and pale,
Whispering tales of days gone by.
In that tranquil, hidden vale,
Stars blend gently with the sky.

Nature's breath, a lullaby,
Cradles life in peaceful sleep.
Underneath that watchful eye,
Promises unspoken keep.

Glimmering Shadows

In the weave of twilight's cloak,
Dancing shadows come to play.
Moonbeams flick, like soft-spun smoke,
Night adorns its grand ballet.

Phantoms glide in spectral grace,
Glimmering under silver light.
Mystery in every face,
In the calm embrace of night.

Whispers carry through the air,
Secrets long since left untold.
Magic lingers everywhere,
Stories spun in whispers bold.

Veiled Gardens

In the veiled, sequestered groves,
Mysteries unfold in hush.
Gentle breeze through petals roves,
Life in tranquil, velvet blush.

Beneath the leaves, a hidden throng,
Creatures weave their secret tales.
Nature hums its ancient song,
Mystic grace between the veils.

Starlight filters through the green,
Lending glow to shadowed nooks.
In this garden, what's unseen,
Speaks in whispers, silent books.

Enfolded Utopia

In the cradle of ancient trees
Where sunlight whispers in the leaves
Dreams unfurl with utmost ease
A world where heartache quietly upheaves

Peaceful streams in silent glide
Reflect the heavens' gentle pride
Nature offers us to confide
In secrets only stars can guide

In every whisper of the wind
A promise of new hope begins
Leaves that twirl in cosmic spin
Most ardent dreams the soul rescinds

Morning dew on petals pure
A taste of life we can't ignore
In this realm, hearts reassure
Enfolds a utopia, evermore

Closeted Eden

Beyond the threshold, secrets kept
A haven where true wonders slept
Inside these walls, no tears were wept
In shadows deep, our spirits leapt

Vines of ivy, thickly grown
Enshroud the paradise unknown
Nature's whispers, softly blown
In silent gardens, overthrown

Birdsong echoes in the morn
In this cradle, dreams are born
From dawn to dusk, till night adorn
An Eden in its hidden form

Fruits that glisten in the sun
Promises of love begun
Wishes granted, one by one
In this closeted Eden, we're as one

Dormant Elysium

Beneath the starlit velvet skies
A land in slumber softly lies
Caressed by echoes, lullabies
A dormant wish where silence flies

Moonlit valleys, shadows play
Guard a beauty kept at bay
Veiled in night's tender embrace
A realm of dreams in patient stay

Whispers weave through ancient air
Secrets linger everywhere
Glimmers soft, beyond compare
A dormant Elysium, rare

Bound by time, in tranquil sleep
Promises we'll always keep
Dreams of stars, serene and deep
In this Elysium, nights gently weep

Hidden Groves

In the sanctum of the woods
Where the heart's pure essence floods
Mystery in every bud
Known to none but the seeking blood

Trails of mossy whispers lead
Where dreams and nature quietly plead
Secret paths the soul must heed
In hidden groves, true hearts are freed

Fern and floral tapestry
Curtains of green, a symphony
Harmony in secrecy
Awaits the soul's deep inquiry

Winding routes of leafy grace
Each step a gentle, pure embrace
Beyond the world, a sacred place
In hidden groves, time's tender trace

Undetected Delight

In shadows soft, where whispers lie,
The moon pours light on night's dark sky,
Silent footsteps through dreams take flight,
In secret spaces, undetected delight.

Stars above in dance so kind,
With threads of silver, they unwind,
Mysteries hidden from morning's sight,
Whispers linger in soft twilight.

Quiet laughter beneath the moon,
In corners where roses bloom,
Hearts untouched by daybreak's light,
Where love whispers undetected delight.

Beneath the veil where dreams intertwine,
In the hush of night, love's design,
In the cloistered dark, a sweet respite,
Where souls awaken to delight.

In the caress of night's embrace,
One finds a world of boundless grace,
A realm unseen, out of sight,
In the heart of undetected delight.

Elusive Elysium

Upon the edge of dawn's first glow,
In dreams of gold, so soft and slow,
Awaits a realm where peace does flow,
The elusive Elysium all hearts know.

Bound by light, each fading star,
We journey close yet stay afar,
In whispers soft, this place we seek,
A paradise where time is meek.

Through veils of mist and morning dew,
The path to bliss, so pure and true,
A fleeting touch, a breath of calm,
Elusive Elysium's gentle balm.

In skies adorned with twilight hues,
A world of calm, in pale blues,
Where hope and dreams and wishes meet,
In Elusive Elysium's retreat.

A place untamed by worldly plight,
In shadows cast by dawn's first light,
An Eden found beyond our sight,
The dream of Elysium takes flight.

Reticent Realm

In dappled light where shadows play,
A hidden world at break of day,
Soft murmurs in the quietude,
The reticent realm of solitude.

By whispering brooks and ancient trees,
A gentle heart finds subtle ease,
In corners where the silence dwells,
Unseen, a realm where peace compels.

The leaves in dance, a silent song,
In this realm where souls belong,
Tender quietude fills the air,
Reticent realm, beyond compare.

In echoes of the winds so mild,
Dreams awaken, spirits wild,
Boundless calm in whispers tell,
The secrets of the reticent realm.

A place where time in stillness lies,
Beneath the watch of azure skies,
In gentle silence, minds unhelm,
Enchanted in the reticent realm.

Mysterious Grove

Within the heart of ancient woods,
Where time is lost, and all withstood,
Mysteries weave through twilight's loom,
In the grove where silent secrets bloom.

Beneath the boughs of green profound,
Where echoes of the past resound,
A whispered breeze, a dance unseen,
In shadows thick with silver sheen.

Hidden pathways wind and wend,
Through realms where dreams and reality blend,
Leaves whisper tales as old as night,
In the mysterious grove's soft light.

By moonlight's kiss and starry gaze,
A world unfolds in twilight's haze,
Mystic moments caught in time,
Where shadows breathe in silent rhyme.

Between the trees, where dreams take flight,
Lies a world of pure delight,
The secrets held, the stories wove,
In the heart of the mysterious grove.

Covert Sanctuary

In shadows deep where dreams collide,
A hidden refuge does reside.
Beneath the cloak of night's embrace,
A sanctuary veiled in grace.

Whispered winds through silent trees,
Carry secrets on the breeze.
Safe within this sacred space,
Find solace in its quiet pace.

Stars above in silent splendor,
Guide the heart, so soft and tender.
Veiled in darkness, peace is sown,
In this covert place unknown.

Latent Serenity

Beneath the surface, calm and still,
A latent peace begins to fill.
In quiet moments, soft as dawn,
Serenity is gently drawn.

Hidden depths where whispers play,
Tell of dreams from far away.
In the quietude, find peace,
Let all turmoil slowly cease.

Rest within this tranquil sphere,
Where silence is a shield, so clear.
Latent blessings, softly bloom,
In this world of quiet room.

Whispered Haven

In the silence of the night,
Whispers weave a soft delight.
Haven found in gentle sound,
Where the spirit is unbound.

Echoes of a distant song,
Carry peace the whole night long.
Rest your mind in tender space,
Where soft whispers interlace.

Moonlight dances on the sea,
Filling hearts with calm so free.
Whispered haven, hidden grace,
Offers peace in this sweet place.

Invisible Bliss

Invisible, yet felt so near,
Bliss surrounds without a fear.
In the moments, quiet, still,
Find the joy, the heart to fill.

Hidden pleasures softly gleam,
Like a secret, precious dream.
Untouched by the sight of man,
Feel the bliss, just as you can.

Gentle laughter, silent song,
In this place, where we belong.
Invisible, yet always here,
Bliss that dries the silent tear.

Unseen Horizon

Beneath the veils of twilight's grace,
Lies a realm where dreams embrace,
Whispers of stars that softly sigh,
Secrets untold in the endless sky.

In shadows deep where hopes entwine,
Paths of wonder we may find,
Mysteries play on the horizon's brim,
As dawn's first light makes edges dim.

Winds of change on silent wings,
Carry the songs the future sings,
Fields of gold in morning's light,
Reveal the dreams held tight at night.

Whispers of dawn so softly grace,
The edge of tomorrow's warm embrace,
In realms unseen, our spirits soar,
To horizons where dreams explore.

Eclectic Sanctuary

In verdant groves where shadows dance,
Find peace in nature's happenstance,
Trees whisper tales of ages past,
In their shade, solace is cast.

A mosaic of life in full array,
Each breath a note in a grand ballet,
Streams murmur secrets to the breeze,
Echoed through the rustling leaves.

Sunlight filters through the canopy,
Crafting patterns, wild and free,
In this sanctuary, hearts align,
In harmony with the divine.

In quiet moments, beauty speaks,
In every nook, in every creak,
An eclectic blend of peace and grace,
In this haven, we find our place.

Hidden Realms

Beneath the world's mundane veneer,
Lies a hidden realm, crystal clear,
Realms where dreams and magic blend,
Mysteries on which hopes depend.

Veiled by night, stars do reveal,
The hidden realms where truths congeal,
Beneath the moon's soft silvery glow,
Wonders thrive in undertows.

Through the shadows, past the known,
Reach the realms where seeds are sown,
In twilight's grace, find hidden doors,
To spaces where imagination soars.

Hear the whispers of the old,
In hidden realms, tales unfold,
In these places, unseen and grand,
Lie the keys to understand.

Latent Elysium

In the silence of a calm divine,
Lies a realm, unseen, sublime,
Latent dreams in shadows bloom,
In the cradle of a twilight room.

Soft echoes of celestial tone,
In Elysium, we are not alone,
A haven where lost souls find,
Peace and solace intertwined.

Whispers of eternity ring,
In latent realms, where angels sing,
Boundless skies and endless seas,
Offer refuge, tranquility perched in trees.

A world unseen by waking eyes,
Yet felt beneath the starry skies,
Latent Elysium in hearts reside,
A sacred place where dreams abide.

Lost Shrine

In the heart of the ancient wood,
Where the fallen leaves lie,
Stands a shrine of forgotten lore,
With secrets in the sky.

Moss-cradled stones tell stories,
Of days and nights gone by,
Echoes whisper through the halls,
Of time that once did fly.

Lanterns no longer gleam,
Their light has long since died,
Only shadows trace the paths,
Where lost spirits abide.

Through the darkened corridors,
Wind sings a mournful tune,
A hymn to souls eternal,
Beneath the ghostly moon.

Once revered, now left behind,
The shrine stands still and cold,
A relic of what time forgot,
Unyielding, brave, and bold.

Enchanted Sanctuary

In a grove where moonlight dances,
Magic fills the air,
Trees whisper ancient incantations,
Beyond the mortal's stare.

Mystic waters gently glisten,
With an ever-glowing light,
Guiding souls to tranquil places,
Safe from darkest night.

Floral scents weave through the air,
Spellbinding those who roam,
In this sanctuary hidden,
Far from hearth and home.

Fairy lights like stars descend,
To grace the soft, green ground,
A realm untouched by sorrow,
Where pure joys can be found.

In this haven, time holds still,
A dreamscape grand and true,
Where hearts find peace eternal,
And hopes are born anew.

Unknown Isles

Beyond the charted waters,
Where the waves do softly speak,
Lie the shores of unknown isles,
Mysterious and unique.

Golden sands kiss ancient rock,
Tides caress every bone,
The whispers of forgotten seas,
Chant melodies alone.

In the depths of mystic caves,
Secrets long buried live,
Legends tell of endless quests,
Of what these lands can give.

Twilight casts an amber blush,
O'er lands untouched by time,
Isles of dreams and wondering eyes,
Compelling and sublime.

Journeys start in silent awe,
To chart the hidden bays,
Where mystery and wonder,
Are the compass for our days.

Shadowed Glades

In the forest's deepest heart,
Where sunlight seldom sees,
Lies the realm of shadowed glades,
Whispered by the breeze.

Darkened paths wind through the gloom,
Where ancient secrets hide,
Shrouded in a moonless night,
The spirits there abide.

Canopies of leaves conspire,
To block the searching light,
Enshrouding all in mystery,
Within the cloak of night.

Songs of owls and rustling leaves,
Compose a haunting tune,
Serenading those who dare,
To wander by the moon.

These glades of darkened beauty,
Hold tales of old and new,
Echoing the timeless dance,
Of shadows we pursue.

Concealed Shangri-La

Beyond the mountains, veiled from the eye,
A haven of peace where dreams take flight,
In whispers of wind the secrets lie,
Under starlit tapestries of night.

Rivers shimmer with liquid gold,
Forests whisper ancient lore,
In this hidden realm, stories unfold,
Of love and beauty evermore.

Footsteps fall on paths unseen,
Guided by heart's true desire,
Beneath the emerald canopy's sheen,
Souls are kindled with ancient fire.

Echoes of laughter through valleys blend,
Eternal joy in hidden streams,
Where time and space together bend,
Fulfilling the most cherished dreams.

This Shangri-La, concealed yet near,
Invites the pure of heart to find,
Its gates unlock through love sincere,
To a paradise unconfined.

Mystic Garden

In the heart of twilight's hold,
Lies a garden, softly veiled,
Of mystic tales that sages told,
Where moon and stars have gently sailed.

Petals blush with secrets kept,
In shadows play the fireflies,
A place where ancient spirits slept,
Beneath the boundless, whispering skies.

Wandering paths by orchid light,
Each step reveals a hidden truth,
Through dreams awoken in the night,
Transcending bounds of age and youth.

Wellspring of the primal sound,
A symphony of life reborn,
In this sacred, hallowed ground,
Of every dusk and every dawn.

To linger here is to conceive,
The essence of life's timeless art,
For in the Mystic Garden's weave,
Lies the core of the human heart.

Invisible Utopia

Beyond the veil of sight and time,
Exists a realm untouched by strife,
A sanctuary of pure rhyme,
Where dreams converge with waking life.

Streets paved with untarnished hope,
Skies are painted hues of peace,
In every heart, the strength to cope,
In every soul, a sweet release.

Invisible to the hurried glance,
Yet felt by those who seek within,
Utopia where virtues dance,
In harmony with the boundless kin.

Mountains whisper songs of grace,
Rivers carve paths of unity,
In every face, a tranquil trace,
Of love and shared community.

This hidden world, for the pure to find,
Invites with open arms so wide,
Invisible to eyes confined,
Yet vivid to the heart's own guide.

Cryptic Sanctuary

In shadows deep where secrets weave,
A sanctuary of cryptic air,
Whispers of past and future cleave,
In silent echoes everywhere.

Labyrinth of ancient stone,
Guardians of forgotten lore,
Its walls are whispers etched in bone,
Unlocking doors to what lies more.

Steps resound through hollow halls,
Glimmers of a world unseen,
Mysteries pulse within these walls,
Where night and understanding convene.

Portals to the realms unknown,
Mirrors to the seeker's mind,
Within this cryptic space alone,
The truths of ages you will find.

So venture forth with spirit bold,
Into the sanctuary deep,
For in its cryptic truth, behold,
The treasures that your soul may keep.

Arcane Meadows

In the hush of twilight, shadows play,
Where dreams in silver softly lay.
Whispers of ancient secrets found,
Among the stars, where hearts unbound.

A gentle breeze through tall green grass,
Echoes of time begin to amass.
Lost in the meadows of arcane delight,
Where moonlit paths reveal the night.

Crickets sing their twilight tune,
Beneath the gaze of the crescent moon.
In the stillness, magic dwells,
In Arcane Meadows, under twilight spells.

Tucked Away Bliss

In a hidden glen, so softly bright,
Lies a realm of golden light.
Where sunlight streams through leaves so green,
And time stands still, a serene dream.

Murmurs of the brook caress the ear,
A whispered song, simple and clear.
In this tucked away, secluded place,
Hearts find solace, in a gentle embrace.

Dappled shadows dance on the ground,
Joy in simplicity, pure and profound.
Here in nature's tender kiss,
We find our peace, our tucked away bliss.

Mirage Gardens

In the dunes where illusions tread,
Gardens bloom in sandy spread.
Petals of mirage, ephemeral grace,
Vanishing in the desert's embrace.

Whispers of the wind carry dreams,
Through arid lands, where sunlight gleams.
Oasis of hope in a barren land,
Mirage Gardens shift like grains of sand.

Cacti and flowers, in fleeting dance,
Form a tapestry of chance.
In the shimmering heat, visions blend,
Where the desert's fantasies never end.

Silent Nirvana

In the stillness of dawn's first light,
Silent whispers take their flight.
Valleys echo with calm divine,
In realms where soul and peace align.

Mountains stand as silent guards,
Nature's beauty, unmarred.
Quietude in the rustling leaves,
Where every heart finds reprieves.

In the quiet, life begins anew,
With silent Nirvana in view.
Here, tranquility's serene embrace,
Holds the world in a tender grace.

Lanterns in the Grove

Among the trees where shadows dance,
Lanterns glow with a mystic trance,
Golden lights on leaves they prance,
Filling hearts with a radiant chance.

The night is young, the air is still,
Whispers echo, the grove they fill,
A gentle breeze with a calming thrill,
As lanterns shine over every hill.

Footsteps soft on a grassy lane,
Stars above in a twinkling chain,
In this grove, no sorrow or pain,
Just lanterns glowing, breaking all strain.

Time flows gently, memories weave,
In lantern light, dreams we retrieve,
In the grove, forever believe,
Magic abounds in what we perceive.

Silent watchers, the trees remain,
In the lantern glow, they never wane,
A fleeting moment, yet they'll retain,
The night where lanterns shone in the lane.

Twilight Oasis

Desert sands when the sun dips low,
Twilight emerges with a gentle glow,
An oasis hidden where shadows grow,
A tranquil place where time is slow.

Palms sway with a whispering breeze,
Stars like jewels through gaps in trees,
The night sings with such gentle ease,
In this twilight, hearts find peace.

Silver waters in moonlit streams,
Reflecting secrets and lovers' dreams,
In this haven, the night redeems,
Offering solace in twilight beams.

Softly murmuring, night birds call,
Echoing within this sacred hall,
In twilight's arms, we feel enthralled,
Away from worries, big and small.

A fleeting realm, this tranquil phase,
Cast in hues of twilight haze,
In this oasis, the soul finds praise,
A gentle respite from worldly craze.

Whispers of Avalon

In the mists where legends lay,
Whispers echo, night turns gray,
Avalon calls in a mystic way,
A dreamscape where old myths sway.

Silver lakes with a glassy sheen,
Forests deep in eternal green,
Echoes of a time once seen,
In Avalon, the soul grows keen.

Knights and maidens, tales retell,
In whispered tones, they weave a spell,
A chime of magic in every dell,
In Avalon, where wonders dwell.

Through the veil where dreams converge,
Whispers guide with a gentle urge,
From Avalon's depths, emotions surge,
In harmony with nature's dirge.

A world apart yet ever near,
Whispers of Avalon, crystal clear,
In every heart, they persevere,
A timeless tale that we revere.

Gossamer Retreat

In the quiet of the dawn's embrace,
Gossamer dreams leave a trace,
A retreat from life's fast pace,
A haven where thoughts interlace.

Morning light on dewdrops play,
Weaving colors in a soft ballet,
In this retreat, fears allay,
As nature's art begins the day.

Whispers soft in a gentle breeze,
Carrying secrets through the trees,
In this place, worries ease,
Replaced by a calm that frees.

Gossamer wings of fleeting time,
Brushing moments so sublime,
In our retreat, life's a rhyme,
Eternal, moving like a chime.

A sanctuary, this precious space,
Gossamer threads entwine with grace,
In every heart, a quiet place,
A retreat where dreams can trace.

Camouflaged Nirvana

In shadows deep, a tranquil lay
Veils of dusk, obscure the day
Where whispers speak, and silence hums
A hidden realm, where solace comes

Amidst the leaves, in nature's fold
A secret peace, serene and bold
In muted tones, the world recedes
A quiet place, where spirit feeds

The twilight's glow, a gentle hand
That guides our souls, to no man's land
Unseen, untouched, the heart finds rest
In camouflaged nirvana's crest

Beneath the stars, so faintly traced
A harmony, in darkness laced
The night conceives, a sacred tale
In shadows, truth and peace prevail

Embrace the dusk, where quiet thrives
In hidden forms, our spirit strives
A camouflaged, ethereal grace
In stillness found, our sacred place

Enshrouded Elysium

A veiled celestial garden lays
Where dreams and whispers intertwine
Enshrouded bliss, in twilight's haze
A quiet realm, with peace divine

Soft aisles of mist, where phantoms tread
Amongst the stars, a silent call
Enshrouded skies, where night's a spread
Of tranquil breaths, that gently fall

A hidden light, the moon's embrace
On tranquil shadow's tender theme
In silence, heartbeats interlace
Within this boundless, starlit dream

Amid the cloaked, eternal night
A symphony of calm unfolds
In shrouded hues, a pure delight
A paradise, the dark enfolds

A land unseen, where spirits soar
In muted rapture's quiet flow
Enshrouded Elysium's core
A secret world for souls to know

Furtive Garden

Beneath the emerald canopy
A hidden bloom in silence grows
In furtive glade, the spirits free
Where whispered winds through petals blow

A tapestry of verdant green
Where shadows dance and secrets play
In furtive garden, sight unseen
A haven where lost dreams can stay

The twilight cloaks in gentle shade
A sanctuary of the heart
In nature's cradle, softly laid
This furtive realm, a work of art

With every leaf, a whispered tale
Of peace found in secluded nooks
Where serenity prevails
In furtive garden's shaded nooks

A hushed repose, a quiet grace
Within this hidden, sacred space
A furtive garden's tender song
Where tranquil souls, in peace belong

Protected Bliss

In secret folds, a tranquil keep
Where dreams and hopes in whispers twine
Protected bliss, where shadows sleep
A refuge for the heart and mind

Amid the dusk, in gentle hues
A haven born from quiet light
Protected from the world's harsh views
In shadows, we escape the night

The silent breath of twilight's kiss
A gentle balm to weary souls
In hidden realms of protected bliss
Where time in peaceful current rolls

Beneath the starlit, quiet skies
A sanctuary safely held
In every shadow, comfort lies
Protected bliss, where calm's compelled

In tranquil depths, our spirits find
A sacred space to rest and mend
Protected bliss, where hearts unwind
In secret solace, without end

Enchanted Refuge

Beneath the canopies high and green,
Whispers of life in shadows seen.
Flowers bloom in silent grace,
Lush serenity, this sacred place.

Silver streams through valleys wind,
Echoes of time, by night confined.
Woodland spirits softly tread,
Guardians of the dreams we've shed.

Twilight beckons, velvet light,
Guides the lost through darkest night.
Stars above, a gleaming cue,
Eyes of old, forever true.

In this haven, hearts take flight,
Dancing free till morning's light.
Every soul finds peace at last,
In the refuge, spells are cast.

Gentle breezes softly sigh,
Kissing leaves as night draws nigh.
Forever safe, our spirits glow,
In this enchanted home we know.

Mystical Utopia

In realms where dreams and wishes blend,
Mystical lands our hearts transcend.
Radiant skies with hues so rare,
Painted worlds beyond compare.

Crystal lakes reflect the sky,
Mirrored depths, where secrets lie.
Mountains touch the heavens high,
Breath of magic in every sigh.

Whispers float on gentle breeze,
Songs of old through ancient trees.
Lush meadows where wonders grow,
Nature's symphony, a gentle flow.

Mystics write on twilight's page,
Tales of love in every age.
Stars align in perfect dance,
Choreographed by purest chance.

Here in this utopian dream,
Every soul finds what they seek.
Boundless realms where spirits soar,
In this enchanted, peaceful shore.

Shrouded Bliss

In twilight's tender, cloaked embrace,
Lies a world we scarce can trace.
Shrouded whispers softly call,
Drawing us where shadows fall.

Veils of mist conceal the light,
Guardian phantoms rule the night.
Secrets held in dark suspense,
A realm beyond our mortal sense.

Luminous glows in hidden glades,
Fireflies weave nature's braids.
Dreams ensnared in night's cool breath,
Lovingly cradled, safe from death.

Midnight winds on quiet streams,
Carry forth our hopes and dreams.
Silent echoes, moonlit moss,
Paths unknown we gently cross.

In this land of shrouded bliss,
Peaceful moments, fleeting kiss.
Lose yourself in twilight's grace,
Find your heart in hidden space.

Concealed Wonderland

Beneath the world, a secret lies,
A hidden realm that softly cries.
Faintest whispers through the trees,
Hush of leaves in secret breeze.

Golden rays through canopies,
Touching down in delicate streams.
Mossy carpets, emerald seams,
Hold the truths of hidden dreams.

Far within, a clearing found,
Where nature's voices softly sound.
Gentle creatures come and go,
In this wonderland we know.

Fragrant blooms of rarest kind,
Perfume the air, our hearts to bind.
Every step in silence takes,
Journey deep for peace's sake.

This sacred place, concealed so well,
A haven where all sorrows quell.
In the heart of nature's hand,
Lies our true, concealed wonderland.

Sequestered Paradise

In a land where whispers fade
Golden hues on twilight's shade
Linger where the moments stray
In sequestered paradise we stay

Whispers of the ancient trees
Mingle with the autumn breeze
Ripples on the tranquil lakes
In sequestered paradise, no heart aches

Stars align in midnight's veil
Silent dreams, a secret trail
Echoes of forgotten times
In sequestered paradise, our rhymes

Gentle waves on silver sands
Hold within, the time's demands
Lost to moments, ever bright
In sequestered paradise, our light

Peaceful nights and endless dawns
Fading where the sun once shone
Caught within a dreamer's gaze
In sequestered paradise, our days

Arcane Bliss

Mystic symbols, shadows cast
Echoed dreams of ages past
Hidden truths in quiet sighs
In arcane bliss, the spirit flies

Moonlit paths of ancient lore
Guard the secrets from before
Whispers cold and timeless kiss
In the depths of arcane bliss

Serenades of silent stars
Mark the trail of untold scars
Found in silence, lost in mist
In the heart of arcane bliss

Veils of night conceal the truth
Fables spun from age to youth
Countless tales and myths persist
In the calm of arcane bliss

Endless realms and hidden doors
Mysteries of nevermore
Life's enigma, ephemeral kiss
Found within arcane bliss

Shadowlands

Beneath the sky of ashen gray
Whispers haunt the light of day
Muffled cries and silent hands
Guide the way in shadowlands

Lonely paths where shadows creep
Guarding secrets, dark and deep
Silent watchers, unseen guides
Lost to time in shadowlands, we hide

Moonlight pales in somber glow
Fleeting tracks where phantoms go
Eternity within our strands
Woven tight in shadowlands

Dusty echoes of the night
Shades of life that lost their light
Phantoms dance in spectral bands
Chained within these shadowlands

Unseen realms and hidden truths
Where twilight sways in spectral booth
In the quiet, still we stand
Embracing all in shadowlands

Eclipsed Eden

In a realm where sun has set
Memories we can't forget
Twilight's curtain, shadows spread
In eclipsed Eden, dreams are fed

Silent whispers of the night
Guide us through the fading light
Faded blossoms, silent trees
In the calm, our senses seized

A cloaked moon in somber sky
Mysteries where wishes lie
Star-lit paths of yonder's call
In eclipsed Eden, we enthrall

Forgotten tales of endless time
Shadows dance in rhythmic rhyme
Echoes of a world undone
In eclipsed Eden, dreams begun

Silent stars and moon's embrace
In this tranquil, sacred place
Lost to night, our spirits blend
In eclipsed Eden, dreams transcend

Latent Blisslands

Upon the nightly dusk, where shadows play,
Silent whispers float, gently, softly sway,
There in hidden realms, dreams fainly sprout,
Echoes of yore, beyond any doubt.

Petals of the moon, in ghostly light,
Guard the secret paths, veiled in night,
Where the heart canst unburden sighs,
Beneath celestial, star-lit skies.

Brook's soft murmur, lullabies the mind,
In the latent blisslands, solace you'll find,
For therein lies an ancient calm,
A river's hymn, an eternal psalm.

The meadows hum, singing songs untold,
In a realm beyond the world's hold,
Lost in tranquil, dreamy mist,
The land where sins are softly kissed.

To roam beneath the timber's shade,
In the silent, moonlit, enchanted glade,
Latent blisslands, keep their quiet grace,
A hidden haven, a soul's lost trace.

Silent Elysium

Where the morning breaks in gentle hues,
Beyond the noise of earthly cues,
Lies a land in tranquil, timeless rest,
A silent Elysium, forever blessed.

Whispers of the breeze, on wings so light,
Carry tales of peace, in the waning night,
To hear the silence, pure and true,
Is to find a world beyond the blue.

Clouds of silver, softly drift and weave,
Nature's symphony, beneath they leave,
In this realm of quiet grace,
Find a haven, a sacred space.

Golden fields, that stretch far wide,
Speak to the heart, an endless tide,
Silent Elysium, a restful shore,
Where the soul finds peace evermore.

With every breath, a soothing balm,
Wrapped in serenity, endless calm,
This silent Elysium, forever stays,
A sanctuary for our mortal days.

Undiscovered Avalon

In dawn's embrace, a whisper speaks,
Of Avalon, where the soul seeks,
Hidden veil, in mystic light,
Undiscovered, out of sight.

Emerald skies and sapphire seas,
Lush meadows kissed by gentle breeze,
Barefoot wander in dreams' domain,
Touch the essence, free from pain.

Forgotten songs in ancient air,
Of Avalon, so pure, so rare,
Blooms of wonder, whispering love,
In secret lands of skies above.

Through the mist, the heart explores,
Undiscovered Avalon's shores,
Echoes of a timeless lore,
Immortality evermore.

Traverse the fields where magic lies,
Gaze upon the boundless skies,
Undiscovered Avalon calls,
A realm where every dream befalls.

Masked Arcadia

Behind the veil of worldly sight,
Lies Arcadia, masked in light,
In whispers of the ancient trees,
Lives the tale of eternal ease.

Fields adorned with morning dew,
Carry secrets, hidden and true,
In the dance of winds, story hides,
Masked Arcadia, where bliss resides.

In the shade of mystic boughs,
Dreams unfold their sacred vows,
To walk in silence, path of grace,
Woven in the secret space.

Cloaked in shades of emerald hue,
A world unseen by many a view,
Masked Arcadia, pure and deep,
Where the weary find their sleep.

Softly tread through verdant lanes,
Where sorrow fades and joy remains,
Unveil the realm of peace so grand,
In Masked Arcadia, forever stand.

Obscured Eden

In shadows deep and rivers wide,
Where tranquil dreams and silence bide,
A hidden world does there reside,
An Eden veiled, our hearts to guide.

Beneath the trees, a twilight hue,
The moon's soft glow, the night anew,
Lost whispers float, the winds accrue,
In mystic realms, a secret view.

The flowers bloom where none can see,
Their fragrances in pure decree,
Enfolded in sweet destiny,
This sacred place, our reverie.

From morning's light to evening's veil,
In every breeze, a secret tale,
Adrift in skies, forever pale,
An Eden here, behind the sail.

In silence, paths of gold revealed,
A treasure trove, in night concealed,
Our senses lost, our fate congealed,
Within this dream, our souls are healed.

Enwrapped Sanctuary

Within the folds of nature's arm,
Lie whispers of a tempered calm,
A world where echoes bring no harm,
In sanctuaries free from alarm.

The winds they speak in gentle tone,
Of lands untouched, by time unknown,
Where mountains guard each sacred stone,
Enwrapped in peace, we are alone.

Through valleys deep and pastures green,
A river winds in tranquil sheen,
Its waters pure, the world serene,
In this embrace, our hearts are seen.

The stars above in night's embrace,
Reveal the cosmos in their grace,
A testament to time and place,
In sacred dreams, we find our space.

In this retreat, the soul's delight,
From dawn's first blush to raven night,
We rest beneath the heavens' sight,
In sanctuaries, forever bright.

Cloistered Haven

Amidst the quiet, hidden nooks,
Where silence wraps in ancient books,
A haven lies, where no one looks,
In cloisters deep, where time forsooks.

The walls they hold old stories keen,
Of whispers soft and sights unseen,
Where echoes past and futures lean,
In shadows cast, a serene keen.

Each pathway twines with secrets dear,
Through corridors, the way is clear,
Protecting all that lingers near,
This hidden realm, devoid of fear.

The gardens bloom in hush profound,
With petals soft that touch the ground,
In sacred stillness all around,
A sanctuary, peace is found.

Above, the sky in vaulted rise,
Watches o'er these sacred ties,
An ancient song within it lies,
In cloistered haven, dreamers' prize.

Cloaked Paradise

Beyond the veil where shadows lie,
A paradise does mystify,
Its secrets cloaked from every eye,
In hidden blooms, the dreams comply.

The morning dew on petals rest,
Each drop a gem upon its crest,
A treasure trove where love's confessed,
In cloaked embrace, our hearts invest.

The forest deep with ancient lore,
Holds mysteries untold before,
In whispered winds through every pore,
This paradise forevermore.

The lakes reflect an endless sky,
Where echoes of the past still fly,
In mirrors deep, our souls espy,
A world unseen by passerby.

In cloaked embrace, we find the key,
To worlds beyond what eyes can see,
In dreams, our spirits wander free,
This hidden realm, our sanctuary be.

Disguised Elysium

Beneath the veil of twilight dim,
Whispers of a hidden hymn,
Where shadows dance in quiet grace,
A paradise, a secret place.

Flowers bloom in twilight's gleam,
Bathed in moonlight's gentle beam,
A world unseen by waking eyes,
Where dreams and reality entwine.

Rivers flow with silken streams,
Echoing ancient, silent dreams,
Mountains rise in soft embrace,
Guardians of this tranquil space.

Birds unseen in twilight's cloak,
Sing melodies that hearts provoke,
In this realm, where time stands still,
Hearts and souls find their will.

Elysium, in disguise so fine,
Calls to spirits, intertwine,
A hidden heaven, pure and bright,
Revealed by only the heart's sight.

Masked Haven

In shadows deep and secrets kept,
A haven waits where sorrows slept,
Masked in darkness, cloaked in night,
It shelters all from storm and fright.

Whispered winds in silent dance,
Offer promises of chance,
Where whispers turn to voices kind,
And troubles, we leave far behind.

In this place of hidden grace,
Masks fall away without a trace,
Here hearts are healed, minds set free,
In tender, loving secrecy.

Haven of the night's embrace,
Gives weary souls a resting place,
In the quiet of the stars,
Lie the mending of our scars.

A masked haven, soft and warm,
Shelters from life's fiercest storm,
In shadows, find your peace anew,
Within its arms, heal and renew.

Phantom Oasis

Amid the desert, dry and wide,
A phantom oasis does hide,
Mirages dance on heat's wild breath,
Whispering life amidst death.

Palms sway with unseen breeze,
Echoes from forgotten seas,
Waters shimmer, cool and clear,
Calling wanderers ever near.

Beneath the blazing sun so fierce,
Soft, sweet refuge, hearts pierce,
Where dreams of shade and rest reside,
In phantom's arms, troubles hide.

Islands of thought in desert's span,
Hold the dreams of every man,
Illusions form what eyes believe,
Oasis real if hearts receive.

A phantom oasis, ever bright,
Guides by faith, beyond sight,
Seek within the arid waste,
Where mirage becomes embrace.

Arcane Eden

In realms where whispers weave their tales,
Arcane Eden quietly prevails,
Magic binds the earth to sky,
Where truth and myst'ry intertwine.

Ancient paths in shadows traced,
Secret gardens, softly placed,
Blooms of knowledge, petals wide,
In this hidden world abide.

Rivers sing in tongues unknown,
Trees with wisdom overgrown,
Stars above in patterns drawn,
Hinting secrets eons long.

Here, the mortal and divine,
Walk as one where fates align,
Woven with enchanted thread,
By the words of ages said.

Arcane Eden, shrouded, pure,
Mysteries forever lure,
Step within and you shall find,
Arcanum of the heart and mind.

Shadowed Eden

In the hush of twilight's grace,
Where whispers meet the twilight's face,
A garden lies in shadows deep,
Where secrets hide and spirits keep.

Leaves that rustle with ancient tales,
Roots entwined like lonesome trails,
Silent echoes of times now past,
In the shadowed Eden, free at last.

Moonlight weaves a silver thread,
Ghostly paths where dreams are led,
Night's embrace, a tender bind,
In this haven of the mind.

Stars above, a watchful eye,
Guardian of the night's soft sigh,
In the shadowed Eden, pure and still,
Hearts find peace and spirits fill.

With dawn's light the shadows fade,
Yet the memories are firmly laid,
In the heart of the shadowed glade,
The Eden where dreams never fade.

Buried Bliss

Underneath the earth's embrace,
Lies a hidden, sacred place,
Where joy once thrived in days of old,
Now stories buried, yet to be told.

Tides of time may wash away,
Surface layers of the day,
But deep below in tranquil peace,
Lingers here the buried bliss.

Roots of life entwine in sleep,
Through the soil they softly creep,
In their grasp, a silent cheer,
Songs of happiness still near.

Glimmers of the life beneath,
In this world of quiet sheath,
Hold the echoes of the past,
In this bliss where dreams hold fast.

Though unseen to naked eye,
In our hearts the truth does lie,
Buried bliss, forever pure,
Earth's deep secrets we endure.

Shrouded Haven

In the veils of mist and cloud,
Where the night sings soft and loud,
A haven shrouded, hidden high,
Reaches out to touch the sky.

Winds that carry whispers old,
Breezes soft with secrets told,
Guardians of this sacred space,
Where time and dreams in silence trace.

Trees bend low with ancient grace,
Shadows dance in rhythmic pace,
Echoes of forgotten days,
In this haven, moonlit bays.

Silver streams through darkened night,
Guide us to this mystic site,
In the shrouded haven's care,
Spirits rise and sorrows pare.

Morning's light may yet reveal,
Truths that night could not conceal,
In the haven softly cast,
Light and dark together last.

Enigmatic Eden

In the realm of mystic dreams,
Where nothing is quite what it seems,
Lies an Eden, lush and wild,
Untamed beauty, undefiled.

Paths that twist and turn with grace,
Leading to a hidden place,
Here the heart may come to rest,
In this Eden deeply blessed.

Clouds that shift in endless dance,
Cloak the world in fleeting trance,
Sun and moon in tandem play,
Light and shadow, night and day.

Whispers of the forest deep,
Guard the tales that secrets keep,
In this enigmatic land,
Time and truth blend hand in hand.

So we wander, lost in thought,
In this Eden, wonders sought,
Mysteries we hope to find,
In the gardens of the mind.

Protected Bliss

In cloistered walls of ancient stone,
Where whispers merge, but never moan,
Safe harbor from the world outside,
In secret's cradle, dreams reside.

Soft lamplight glows on velvet night,
While shadows cast a gentle fright,
Guardians of this hallowed space,
Ensuring peace shall leave no trace.

The essence of a silent pact,
Through quiet oaths, the bonds intact,
In stillness, serenades deploy,
A gentle hum of guarded joy.

Ensconced in layers, thick and warm,
Sheltered from life's grievous storm,
Elysian fields within these walls,
Protective veil that softly falls.

Here, time itself does softly cease,
Entrapped within this blissful peace,
The soul finds solace, ease, and song,
In cloistered arms, where hearts belong.

Unknown Haven

Beyond the map where charts expire,
Lies a haven draped in silver wire,
Emerald paths through shadow's lee,
A hermit's wish, a soul set free.

Guardians veiled in twilight's gray,
Protect the hearts who choose to stay,
In labyrinths of silent lore,
Where dreams descend to seek and soar.

Mystic winds through ivy weave,
Secrets that the mind receives,
In stillness deep and twilight dim,
A tranquil hymn, a whispered hymn.

Riddles carved on ancient bark,
Hidden truths in realms of dark,
A respite from the world's embrace,
In the unseen, a sacred space.

Calm descends like morning dew,
In this haven, ever true,
Sanctuary, a soul unchained,
Where peace and quiet are sustained.

Hushed Gardens

In gardens hushed with silent sighs,
Where secret tales do softly lie,
Each petal whispers bygone dreams,
In moonlit nights, where starlight gleams.

Among the roots of ancient trees,
Lie secrets carried by the breeze,
In blooms that never speak aloud,
Silent songs, a fragrant shroud.

Wander through these sacred groves,
Where time in quiet circle roves,
The heart finds peace in muted hues,
In silken air, a gentler muse.

Hidden paths with ivy dressed,
Lead to nooks where souls can rest,
Each step within this hallowed ground,
A promise kept, a love profound.

Beneath the sky's embrace of blue,
In gardens hushed, where dreams accrue,
The quiet whispers of the night,
A symphony of pure delight.

Secreted Blissland

In a land where shadows cast no form,
Where hearts are shielded from the storm,
Lies a bliss that none can see,
A refuge carved in mystery.

Veiled in twilight's tender glow,
Paths meander, soft and slow,
Each footfall echoes calm and grace,
In this secreted, sacred place.

Here the winds sing lullabies,
Beneath the sun's whispered goodbyes,
In each breath, a tranquil chord,
In blissland, joy's reward.

Life's burdens cease to weigh and strain,
Within this realm, no grief or pain,
Just melodies of peace and light,
A softened haven, pure and bright.

Encased in nature's fond embrace,
Time dissolves without a trace,
In secreted blissland's tender fold,
Eternal peace, a dream retold.

Dusky Haven

In the dusky haven's glaze,
Where twilight whispers softly,
The skies are painted purple hues,
And shadows dance most loftily.

The river hums a quiet tune,
Its waters cool and deep,
Reflecting heavens far above,
As stars begin to peep.

Whispers of the night unfold,
Secrets old and wise,
In this haven, dusk remains,
Beneath the velvet skies.

The world, it seems, is hushed away,
In moments strangely rare,
For in this dusky haven's hold,
There's magic in the air.

Veiled Enchantment

Beneath the night's enfolding cloak,
Where moonlight weaves its spell,
A realm of veiled enchantment lies,
Where secrets softly dwell.

The forest whispers ancient tales,
Through trees with silver leaves,
And in this mystic twilight veil,
A heart of magic breathes.

Lanterns glow with tender light,
Like fireflies in the shade,
Guiding souls through paths unseen,
Where dreams, for now, are made.

Each step into this gentle night,
Unveils a secret space,
Where veiled enchantment calls aloud,
Inviting warm embrace.

Enchanted Delve

In the heart of ancient woods,
Where sunlight scarcely beams,
Lies the enchanted delve unseen,
A kept place in our dreams.

With every step, a whisper heard,
From creatures small and fae,
They dance in circles, silently,
Throughout the dusky day.

Rivers weave like silver threads,
Through emerald tapestry,
And every leaf within this grove,
Holds a whispered mystery.

The deeper in this delve we tread,
The more the heart unfurls,
For in the enchanted woodlands' soul,
Lie countless hidden worlds.

The Quiet Beyond

Beyond the noise and hurried pace,
Past the rush and ceaseless stare,
Lies a quiet, hidden place,
With peace held in its air.

The quiet beyond calls clear and soft,
A whisper in the night,
Leading hearts to gently cross,
Into a realm of light.

Silence sings a soothing song,
To souls that seek a rest,
In the quiet, shadows long,
Are softened and caressed.

Here, time itself will slow its hand,
Each moment gently spreads,
In the quiet beyond the land,
Where peace unfolds its threads.

Disguised Splendor

Amid the fog, there lies a dream,
In shadowed hues that softly gleam.
A mystic charm, concealed in flight,
A world adorned in twilight's light.

Whispers weave through silken air,
Enigmas dance, elusive, rare.
In hidden realms where wonders flow,
The veil that lifts where secrets glow.

Masked by drapes of midnight's cloak,
The stars ignite with words unspoke.
Gleaming constellations, bright,
Illuminate the hushed delight.

Beneath the whispering night sky,
A silent symphony sings nigh.
The splendor guards its mystic gate,
With visions grand and moments great.

Thus beauty cloaked in mist and mire,
In quietude, it sparks desire.
Wrapped in glamour, hushed and pure,
Disguised splendor shall endure.

Hidden Glades

In the forest, deep and still,
Lies a world where dreams fulfill.
A secret grove, untouched by time,
Where nature sings in perfect rhyme.

Sunlight filters through the leaves,
Dancing shadows it achieves.
Birdsong whispers on the breeze,
Harmonies that hearts appease.

Paths are winding, mossy green,
Leading to enchanted scene.
Flowers bloom in vibrant show,
In hidden glades where rivers flow.

Mystery in each petal's sway,
Nature's secrets on display.
A haven where the soul retreats,
In silent reverence, heartbeats.

Hidden glades, a refuge grand,
A sanctuary tucked in land.
Peaceful solace, beauty true,
Eternally, it waits for you.

Veiled Nirvana

Past the clouds, through skies untold,
Lies a realm of myths and gold.
Veiled Nirvana, pure and bright,
Shrouded in celestial light.

Harmony in ether drifts,
A sanctuary that uplifts.
Silent whispers, tender grace,
In this hidden, sacred place.

Mountains rise with dignity,
Guardians of serenity.
Streams of silver, moonlit beams,
Weaving through, as if in dreams.

Timeless peace in cosmic flow,
In this haven, love does grow.
Every soul that finds its way,
Fades into the light of day.

Veiled Nirvana, endless gleam,
Where the heart can find its dream.
Eternally, it calls in song,
To realms where spirits do belong.

Furtive Eden

Softly tread where shadows play,
In a realm where secrets lay.
Furtive Eden, hidden vale,
Where whispered winds begin to sail.

Verdant leaves in quiet hush,
Wake beneath the twilight's blush.
Mystic garden, cloaked with care,
Dreams and whispers linger there.

Petals fold in tranquil night,
Glow beneath the moon's soft light.
Rosy dawn and dusky eve,
A sanctuary we perceive.

Nature's voice in silent hymn,
Golden light on waters dim.
Echoes of a world concealed,
In Furtive Eden, all revealed.

Furtive Eden, peaceful, calm,
Cradling hearts within its palm.
A paradise of subtle grace,
In hidden realms, find your place.

Ebony Meadows

In ebony meadows, whispers of night,
The moon casts shadows, silver and light,
Stars glisten softly, a celestial flight,
Silent serenades of secret delight.

A breeze caressing the darkened earth,
In dreams, we wander, seeking rebirth,
The past and future in twilight's mirth,
Life's endless cycle, death's gentle girth.

Crickets play the symphony, nature's tune,
Beneath the gaze of a silent moon,
Dreams are woven in night's cocoon,
In ebony meadows, midnight soon.

Petals of darkness, a fragrant plea,
Boundless sky, the soul let free,
In the heart of night, eternity,
We find our place, our destiny.

Through the silence, a heartbeat flows,
In realms where the night wind blows,
Peace in darkness, where no one knows,
In the endless dance of ebony meadows.

Uncharted Eden

In uncharted Eden, wild and free,
Verdant paths beneath ancient trees,
Birdsong whispers secrets to the breeze,
A paradise found in mysteries.

Rivers of gold where sunlight streams,
Mirrors of life, reflecting dreams,
Echoes of laughter where joy redeems,
Boundless love in nature's schemes.

Petals vibrant in colors ablaze,
In Eden's garden, forever stays,
The heart unburdened, lost in a daze,
Where time stands still in nature's praise.

Mountains stand tall, guardians grand,
With horizons kissed by creator's hand,
Each moment sacred, a promise planned,
In uncharted Eden, where we stand.

Veils of dawn in soft embrace,
Each shadow a brushstroke of grace,
In the heart of Eden's gentle place,
We find our truth, our rightful space.

Luminous Shadows

In luminous shadows, light meets dark,
An interplay, a timeless ark,
Bright whispers, the night does mark,
A silent song, a hidden spark.

Celestial beams dance in disguise,
Beneath the veil of twilight skies,
An ephemeral glance, a fleeting reprise,
Of dreams that in night arise.

Stars paint the sky in spectral glow,
A cosmic ballet in gentle flow,
Secrets of the universe to bestow,
In luminous shadows casting shallow.

Through the twilight, the unknown calls,
In the interplay, inspiration falls,
Between light and dark, a lace of walls,
An eternal dance within night's halls.

Mystery and clarity intertwined,
In shadowed light, the soul defined,
In quiet whispers, our truths we find,
In luminous shadows, forever aligned.

Forbidden Grove

In the forbidden grove, secrets deep,
Shadowed canopies, a silence sleek,
Whispers of ancient trees that keep,
Stories buried in memories' sleep.

Moonlight filters through velvet leaves,
A dance of light where darkness heaves,
An essence of wonder, magic weaves,
In the air, where the heart believes.

Paths untrodden by mortal feet,
Where the echoes of the old world meet,
Silent guardians, a timeless beat,
In the grove where shadows retreat.

Mystic beings in twilight's mist,
In sacred places, angels kissed,
The grove's enchantment, hard to resist,
A realm where dreams and reality twist.

Here, under boughs of emerald shade,
The forbidden grove where fortunes are made,
In the heart of secrets, unafraid,
We find our truth, our spirits' aid.

Cryptic Sanctuary

In shadows deep, where secrets lie,
The silent winds in whispers sigh,
A realm concealed from prying eyes,
Where moon and stars dare not arise.

Forgotten tales in twilight slumber,
Ancient runes that time encumber,
Ethereal doors, a mystic flair,
Guardians of the sacred lair.

Echoes drift in spectral tunes,
Through corridors of phantom ruins,
Lost beneath the midnight's cloak,
Enigmas in the darkness spoke.

Veiled realms of the long forsaken,
By cryptic dreams their ties unshaken,
Silent oaths in whispers steep,
Guard this hidden world so deep.

In the dusk of brume and blight,
Secrets bloom in endless night,
A hallowed sanctuary, ageless and true,
Unknown marvels it does construe.

Subterranean Haven

Beneath the earth where shadows sleep,
In caverns dark and silence deep,
A secret world of hidden light,
Shelters from the day and night.

Crystals gleam in dim retreats,
In whispered tones, the stillness speaks,
Rivers flow beneath the stone,
A haven where the heart is known.

Mossy walls with history veined,
Untold tales in rock engrained,
Echoes of the surface gone,
Life in quiet, moving on.

Roots of trees above descend,
Finding pathways to extend,
Life in darkness, thriving still,
Subterranean, soft and still.

Safe from storms and winter's chill,
In the earth's deep heart they dwell,
A haven carved in secret halls,
Where time, unnoticed, softly falls.

Peace prevails in this domain,
A world apart, where hushed remain,
A sanctuary, earth's warm embrace,
Subterranean, a sacred place.

Lush Veil

Underneath a verdant shroud,
Where sunbeams pierce through leaf and cloud,
A canopy of green so tall,
Shelters creatures great and small.

Whispers weave through emerald trees,
Dancing with the fragrant breeze,
Nature's breath in song divine,
A tapestry of life entwined.

Mysteries in shadows play,
In the cool embrace of day,
Vines that twine in secret bowers,
Blooming forth with unseen flowers.

Water's song in hidden streams,
Serenades the forest dreams,
Pools of peace where spirits dwell,
In this lush and leafy shell.

Timeless realm where life prevails,
In the hush of ancient tales,
In the veil, so rich and green,
A sanctuary, serene and keen.

Sheltered Eden

In the heart of leafy bower,
Blossoms bloom with every hour,
Softly cradled by the shade,
In Eden's arms, all fears evade.

Birds of color, songs divine,
Echo through the verdant shrine,
Where sunlight whispers through the leaves,
And every soul, in peace, believes.

Deer do graze on emerald pastures,
Bound by nature's gentle master,
Streams that glisten, crystal clear,
Flowing with the joy that's near.

Gardens kissed by morning dew,
In every petal, life anew,
A landscape painted with repose,
Where every bud in solace grows.

In this haven, wild and free,
Harbors life's tranquility,
Sheltered Eden, pure and bright,
Cradles all in calm delight.

Camouflaged Zenith

In clouds where secrets softly sleep,
Beyond the crest of twilight's sweep,
A zenith hides in veiled array,
Where whispers of the stars will play.

A summit cloaked in sun's embrace,
Shadows dance with a gentle grace,
The peak unseen, yet near to heart,
In every whispered breeze, a part.

Through mists and echoes, dreams ascend,
Toward the sky where visions blend,
Camouflaged yet reaching high,
A peak unseen by mortal eye.

In twilight's veil, it bids us near,
A silent call that's always here,
The zenith waits in masked repose,
A mystery the night bestows.

A hidden apex, still and grand,
Where heavens touch the shadowed land,
And in the dark, its light revealed,
In dreams, the zenith is unsealed.

Arcane Enclave

Within the fold of ancient lore,
A sanctum where the spirits soar,
Arcane glyphs the walls adorn,
Where secrets of the old are born.

Whispers weave through time and space,
Mystic hymns in this secret place,
Enclaves of the mind and soul,
Where hidden truths unite, make whole.

Candles flicker, shadows sway,
Guardians of the night and day,
Runes inscribed in silent lore,
Enigma's touch on every door.

In the hush of twilight's breath,
Lies the knowledge life and death,
Arcane paths the wise have tread,
Echoes of the thoughts unsaid.

A realm where wisdom folds and bends,
Beyond the grasp of foe or friends,
In this enclave, the arcane thrives,
Preserving secrets of past lives.

Secluded Splendor

A hidden grove where silence sings,
With secret paths and whisperings,
Beneath the boughs, the daylight glows,
A world where time itself slows.

Enclosed in nature's soft embrace,
A refuge from the outer grace,
Secluded meadows gently bloom,
Dispelling shadows, gloom to plume.

In shaded glades where dreams are made,
The heart finds peace, its worries fade,
Splendor tucked away from sight,
In the quiet, pure delight.

Streams murmur soft with tales of old,
Mountains whisper wealth untold,
In this seclusion, life unfolds,
Beauty bound in nature's hold.

A sanctuary of the land,
Where tranquil thoughts and spirits stand,
In splendor's gentle, quiet reign,
The soul's own secrets here remain.

Secretive Arcadia

In depths of forests dense and green,
A haven of the unseen,
Arcadia whispers on the breeze,
A secret place of ancient trees.

Hidden pathways lead the way,
To lands where night kisses the day,
In shadows cast by giant oaks,
Are tales untold by forest folks.

Among the leaves, the spirits play,
Guardians of this sacred bay,
Where dreams and fables intertwine,
Beneath the shade of spruce and pine.

In twilight hours, soft and mild,
Arcadia's secrets run wild,
Silent hymns of earth and sky,
In this realm where echoes lie.

A sanctuary, lost in time,
Where nature's hush becomes a rhyme,
In secretive embrace, sublime,
Arcadia keeps its prime.

Lost Sanctuary

In the heart of twilight's gleam,
Whispers of a distant dream.
Shadows dance, shadows sigh,
Underneath a forlorn sky.

Ancient walls of time now frail,
Echoes of a mournful tale.
Once a haven, now adrift,
Spirits wander, memories lift.

Silent steps on cobblestone,
Echoes of a life unknown.
Through the mist and through the haze,
Lost in time's unending maze.

Ghostly figures, soft and pale,
Guard the secrets, cold and stale.
In this sanctuary, lost,
Wandering souls, tempest-tossed.

Find me in the twilight's glow,
Where the haunted shrubs do grow.
Seek the solace, find the pain,
In this world, we roam in vain.

Secret Glories

Hidden paths in forest deep,
Whisper secrets while we sleep.
Underneath the ancient trees,
Lies the magic, sure to please.

Mystic rivers, crystal clear,
Songs of ancient days revere.
Lanterns float upon the stream,
Lighting up a secret dream.

Keepers of the hidden truth,
Serenades from distant youth.
Guardians of dusk and dawn,
Mysteries that linger long.

Stars align in perfect dance,
Giving life a fleeting chance.
In these glories, silent, still,
Hearts and dreams, they interfill.

Find the tales in moonlit glen,
Secret glories known to men.
In the shadows, in the light,
Whispers long into the night.

Elusive Blisslands

Far beyond the mortal's grasp,
In a realm where dreams do clasp.
Lies a land of whispered breeze,
Hidden 'neath the willow trees.

Hopes and dreams, like fireflies,
Glowing under velvet skies.
Fields of gold and rivers bright,
Embrace the warmth of endless night.

Silent songs and ancient lore,
Guide the hearts forevermore.
Seek the path where blisses reign,
Journey through the sweet refrain.

In these lands, the soul finds peace,
World of wonders, sweet release.
Elusive yet so close at hand,
Wander in this blissful land.

Veil of shadows, lift once more,
Reveal the joys we search for.
Blisslands calm the weary mind,
In its arms, true peace we find.

Cloaked Utopia

Shrouded in the mystic veil,
Utopia where dreams prevail.
Hidden from the world's disdain,
Lies a place devoid of pain.

Gardens filled with endless bloom,
Fragrant night, dispelling gloom.
Wisps of light, a golden hue,
Show the path for chosen few.

Harmony in every breath,
Peace that conquers life and death.
Cloaked beneath a tender sky,
Where the soul can freely fly.

Waters pure and twilight's grace,
Fill the heart, a blessed place.
Softly hums the tranquil plea,
In this land, we long to be.

Seek the veil, unearth the door,
Find the haven, evermore.
Cloaked Utopia awaits,
Destiny within our fates.

Celestial Hideout

In the night, where stars ignite,
A hidden realm takes its flight.
Far beyond the moon's soft glow,
Secrets in the sky, they flow.

Whispers in the midnight breeze,
Speak of calm and gentle ease.
Where dreams paint the cosmic art,
And the mind and spirit part.

Silent echoes of the past,
In the void of space at last.
Unseen worlds, a boundless sphere,
Hold their mysteries near.

Galaxies whisper through time,
In this celestial climb.
A sanctuary up so high,
In the blanket of the sky.

Let your spirit find its way,
Where the night outlasts the day.
In this secret, starry lane,
Peace and wonder ever reign.

Secret Oasis

Beyond the dunes, where silence speaks,
A paradise in sand's fair streaks.
An emerald pool, a life's embrace,
Holds mystery in its hidden space.

Palm trees dance with gentle grace,
In this secluded, sacred place.
Whispering winds, they gently brush,
In the quiet, calm and hush.

Sunlight filters, warm and bright,
Turning day to golden light.
In shadows cool, a safe retreat,
Where earth and heaven meet.

Crystal waters softly sing,
In this desert's secret spring.
Life, it blossoms in the dry,
Reaching to the azure sky.

Here, the soul finds calm and ease,
Amongst the sands and whispering trees.
A haven hidden from the strife,
In the cradle of life.

Peace and wonder, they reside,
In this tranquil, desert tide.
A secret hidden, safe and sound,
In the beauty of the ground.

Veiled Haven

Through mist and shadow, softly tread,
Where unseen paths are gently led.
A hidden nook, where silence stays,
In a realm of twilight haze.

Whispers drift through ancient trees,
Echoing with timeless ease.
In the quiet, find your cheer,
As the calm draws ever near.

Veiled by branches, safe and sound,
Nature's secrets here are found.
In the hush of forest's call,
Let the peaceful moments fall.

Streams that murmur, leaves that sigh,
In this nook, the heart can fly.
Where the world fades softly out,
And the soul can roam about.

Softly tread within this space,
Find the quiet, find your grace.
In this veiled haven's light,
Rest and dream through the night.

Unknown Eden

Beneath the skies of endless blue,
Lies a land both known and new.
Untouched by time's unyielding hand,
An Eden in this quiet land.

Flowers bloom in vibrant hues,
Greens and golds of countless views.
Whispered winds through branches sway,
In this timeless, bright array.

Waterfalls in endless play,
Crafting songs both night and day.
Birds that sing and hearts that soar,
In this haven evermore.

Wander through this verdant realm,
Where love and peace at last helm.
Each footstep calls to rest and peace,
In this place, all conflicts cease.

Let your worries fade and fall,
In this Eden, hear the call.
Unveil the dreams within the heart,
In this land, a brand new start.

Find your shelter, find your grace,
In the warmth of nature's face.
This unknown Eden, pure and bright,
Guides us through the quiet night.

Whispers of Eden

Where waters cool and winds are kind,
In realms where dreams and day entwine,
Here whispers soft like elven song,
Weave tales of gardens lost in time.

A dance of leaves, a symphony,
Of olden days and mysteries,
Eden's whispers secrets hold,
Of timeless beauty, tales retold.

In shadows cast by ancient trees,
Where dawn's light breaks upon the leaves,
Life's gentle breath does softly play,
In Eden's realm, where spirits sway.

Let hearts be light and spirits free,
Inspired by this reverie,
In whispers of a time divine,
Where Eden's dreams and hope align.

The Veiled Haven

In twilight's kiss, where shadows grow,
A haven veiled in twilight's glow,
With secrets woven in the night,
A refuge from the worldly woe.

Where whispers ride on moonlit breeze,
And stars paint stories through the trees,
A sanctuary for the heart,
A place where souls can find release.

Underneath the ancient sky,
Where silent dreams and truths reside,
The Veiled Haven calls us all,
To rest and in its grace abide.

A hidden world, a silent call,
In dreams the Veiled Haven falls,
A refuge wrapped in night's embrace,
Where weary spirits can find grace.

Secret Gardens

Behind the walls where ivy twists,
Lie secret gardens wrapped in mist,
A world where only few have tread,
To find the magic that persists.

In every petal, whisper blooms,
With tales of old and ancient runes,
A sanctuary, lush and wild,
In gardens where the spirit swoons.

Paths of moss and hidden streams,
Reflect the light of bygone dreams,
Each blossom holds a mystery,
Unveiling truths in twilight's gleam.

Secret gardens, hearts' delight,
A refuge in the morning light,
Here within the whispered pines,
Where nature's secrets intertwine.

Cloaked Sanctuary

Within the cloak of shadows deep,
A sanctuary stirs in sleep,
A place where dreams and quiet meet,
In hidden groves, so still and sweet.

Beneath the canopy, so grand,
In realms of whispering woodland,
A refuge built by nature's hand,
For weary souls to understand.

Amongst the ferns and timeless trees,
Where silence hums with ancient ease,
A hidden world of peace and calm,
A restful balm upon the breeze.

Cloaked Sanctuary, soft and warm,
Where hearts can weather any storm,
A shelter from the world's demand,
This sacred space, by nature planned.

Serene Cocoon

In silence, whispers softly loom,
A gentle hum, a soulful tune,
Wrapped in warmth, a soft, sweet swoon,
In the heart of a serene cocoon.

Moonlight bathes in silver streams,
Dancing on the quilted seams,
Nighttime breathes with quiet dreams,
In the folds of a serene cocoon.

Gentle wings cupped in rest,
Nature's grace in her best,
Cradled close, forever blessed,
In the lap of a serene cocoon.

Soft winds whisper 'cross the grove,
Tenderly in velvet rove,
A tranquil place where spirits strove,
In the arms of a serene cocoon.

Heartbeats echo in this lair,
Life's simple chords laid bare,
In comfort's weave, beyond compare,
In the warmth of a serene cocoon.

Enigmatic Shelter

Mystery in the shadows lie,
A haven bold beneath the sky,
In quiet realms where spirits fly,
In the enigmatic shelter nigh.

Questions drift like leaves in breeze,
A cryptic dance amid the trees,
Secrets whispered to the seas,
In the enigmatic shelter please.

Heartbeats sync with nature's song,
Strange and wondrous, echoes long,
In this place where we belong,
In the enigmatic shelter strong.

Comfort found in hidden folds,
Ancient tales that time upholds,
Bound in wonders, secrets told,
In the enigmatic shelter's hold.

Here we find our sacred space,
Mystic whispers, soft embrace,
Timeless bonds in fleeting grace,
In the enigmatic shelter's place.

The Tucked Away

In shadows deep, away we stay,
A quiet breath, the world at bay,
Peaceful moments, night and day,
Within the realm of the tucked away.

Beneath the veil, the whispers play,
Soft caresses, gentle sway,
Hidden places where dreams lay,
In the corners of the tucked away.

Light filtered through a leafy screen,
A secret world, a hidden scene,
Where life's magic we can glean,
In the depths of the tucked away serene.

Echoes of the past reside,
In the nooks where moments hide,
Silent rivers softly glide,
In the calm of the tucked away inside.

Here we find a sacred rest,
In the fold of nature's vest,
Cradled close, forever blessed,
In the heart of the tucked away's quest.

Starlit Enclave

Beneath the dome of infinite night,
Stars assemble in their rite,
Midnight canvas glows so bright,
In the arms of a starlit enclave's light.

Constellations weave a tale,
Cosmic threads in night's own veil,
Guided by a starship's sail,
In the hold of a starlit enclave's trail.

Galaxies in whispered sound,
Circles dance in endless round,
Feet in sky and heart unbound,
In the space of a starlit enclave found.

Crystals gleam in silent vast,
Time forgotten, present, past,
Starry moments gently cast,
In the hush of a starlit enclave's grasp.

Heaven's secrets softly sing,
Echoes of an angel's wing,
Peace and wonder they do bring,
In the grace of a starlit enclave's ring.

Cloaked Haven

Beneath the ancient willow's shade,
In whispers, secrets softly laid,
A refuge from the world we weave,
A haven cloaked where hearts can grieve.

Shadows dance on dusky leaves,
Silent hymns the evening weaves,
Breaths converge as hearts unfold,
In the twilight, stories told.

Moonlight filters through the veil,
Casting dreams on cloud and trail,
Echoes hum where silence calls,
In this cloaked, serene hall.

Crickets sing their lonesome tune,
Underneath the silvered moon,
Time suspends its ceaseless race,
Held within this hidden place.

A refuge crafted from our pain,
Where loss can cleanse like gentle rain,
In the sanctuary, soft and warm,
Sheltered from the storm's arm.

Veiled Splendors

Veiled in mist, the morning rises,
Secrets held in thin disguises,
Golden light through fog descends,
With hidden beauty, day begins.

Whispers on the morning breeze,
Unseen wonders among the trees,
Nature's canvas cloaked in grace,
In veiled splendors, we find our place.

Shadows play in corners dark,
Leaving whispers, subtle marks,
A dance of light no eye can trace,
In this obscured, divine embrace.

Stars that fade as dawn awakens,
Hold their mysteries, never shaken,
Veiled splendors in twilight blend,
Where dreams and day begin to mend.

The world in shades of grey and gold,
Veils of splendor stories told,
Through the mist and light combined,
We glimpse the truths we strive to find.

Milton Keynes UK
Ingram Content Group UK Ltd.
UKHW050028190624
444315UK00015B/844

9 789916 756218